D1581715

Fall

A Play

James Saunders

Samuel French — London
New York — Sydney — Toronto — Hollywood

FALL

Presented at the Hampstead Theatre on 6th September 1984 with the following cast:

Roche (Fox)	Roland Oliver
Ann	Sylvestra le Touzel
Helen	Julie Covington
Kate	Cecily Hobbs
Mary	Gwen Watford

Directed by	Robin Lefevre
Decor	Sue Plummer
Lighting	Leo Leibovici

The play is set in a suburban garden on an afternoon in late summer

Time: the present

ACT ONE*

A suburban garden. A Sunday afternoon in late summer

A garden table, holding an almost empty bottle of wine, four glasses and one or two things left uncleared from a cold meal: a side-plate or two, perhaps, and cheese. Four garden chairs. The light is as sunlight

Fox A garden ... A table ... Sun .... Late afternoon sun, late summer, an unforeseen late summer ... A Sunday, a table in a garden one late summer late Sunday afternoon. On it: wine bottle, glasses, remnants of a late alfresco lunch ...

Ann enters, as from the end of the garden. She is heavily pregnant. In the palm of one hand she carries some plums. She stands at the table, puts the plums on it, pours some wine into a glass, drinks, and sits down. Fox watches her

A post-prandial, post late prandial late summer late afternoon unexpectedly sunny Sunday garden. Into which Ann, pregnant, enters; as one says. Was in fact, we are to assume, out of sight among the fruit trees at the end of the garden but for our purposes enters, pregnant. Carrying carefully a handful of—plums; and her baby. To be. Or not to be.

Ann puts her face up to the sun, closes her eyes, sighs

She has returned to the parental home this sunny late summer weekend, as have her two sisters, to attend the dying of their father. The sisters will appear, as will the mother. Together and separately, between passing to and from the house and the end of the garden on various errands, they will discuss various topics, general and particular, for an acceptable length of time, then all will be as it was before ...

Ann sits face upturned to the sun, eyes closed

Ann lives in a squat in—Bristol. The putative father-to-be, a kind of musician, lives with her, when he is not elsewhere. Consider an analogy between the way she inhabits her squat and the way she inhabits her body. She'd not pretend to own it. "Property is theft"—Proudhon. "Property is a mausoleum for the living dead"—Norman O. Brown. It becomes, while she uses it, part of her. Not an extension of her, that would suppose a centre capable of extension. She is what she inhabits, while she inhabits it. She dwells, one might say, in an elasticated self in a continuous present ... The baby, of course, is an accident, though she'd not admit to it. That is to say, she'd not accept the validity of the term. Accident and design are two facets of the same coin, which seem

---

* N.B. Paragraph 3 on p. ii of this Acting Edition regarding photocopying and video-recording should be carefully read.

to us opposites because of a peculiarity of our mental vision. All is in fact both deliberate and accidental and all is for the best; or, since best and worst are but two facets of the same coin, for the worst. The baby, we may say, was not planned. Or rather, she did not plan the baby. Or rather, she did not consciously plan the baby. Does she want it? She wants what is. It is, therefore she wants it—she would say.

Helen enters from the house, carrying a paperback

Helen I thought you were going to help with the washing up. (*She sits, opens the paperback and finds her place*)

Ann I said to leave it. I said I'd do it.

Helen It's done now.

Ann Where's the mother?

Helen Still up there ... I just didn't want her to come down and see it there. She'd have done it. I don't see why she should have to.

Ann She wouldn't have to. I was going to do it.

Helen She'd have done it. You know that.

Ann Maybe it'd be better than doing nothing.

Helen You obviously didn't think so.

Ann I was talking about her.

Slight pause

Anyway she didn't come down and you've done it so that's all right, isn't it?

Helen puts the book down. She picks up the wine bottle and pours what's left, very little, into her glass

Have you been in to see him?

Helen No. They were talking. At least Mum was.

Ann He's conscious then.

Helen I don't know.

Fox Helen, once married, now not. Embraced, with her former husband, a left-wing variety of the psychotherapeutic faith. Lost the faith but keeps the form, more or less. Lives and works now in a shoestring hostel for the socially inadequate in—Wandsworth; whom she feeds soup, Marx and self-respect; as the Salvation Army feeds soup, Christ and humility.

Helen I wish he'd go.

Ann looks at her

It would be better. He's drugged to the eyeballs ... It seems such a humiliation ... Mum talks to him all the time when she's up there. She tells him the events of the day, you know, all the little trivia: what who said, what who's wearing. About the cowboy who called with the manure, from some stables. What Bob Gunnell said when he saw it. Straw and piss, straw and piss ... I don't think he hears, he doesn't register.

Ann You don't know what he hears.

Helen I know he's got enough morphine in him to sink a battleship.

Pause

Ann Where's Kate?

Helen She was in the lav last time I saw her.

Ann Saw her?

Helen Heard her.

Ann giggles

Ann Oh, well, she'll be an hour or two. (*Seriously*) She goes to the loo an awful lot, doesn't she?

Helen I hadn't noticed.

Ann Haven't you? She's always at it. You're in the middle of a conversation on some burning topic and suddenly she rushes off to the loo ... Maybe she does her contemplation in there; says her mantra between plops, like telling beads ... Did you know she's got a guru?

Helen Get away.

Ann Well, an amateur one. I mean he's not a black belt or anything. Not even Indian, he's a Kraut. One of her weird circle.

Helen You can talk of weird circles.

Ann At least we've got past *self-improvement*. Jesus ...

Helen Evidently.

Ann What? Oh, I see, ha ha ... They call him the Master. "Meister", they call him ... They *do*. He's got fuzzy hair and sandals and he only says about ten words a day in case he might not be profound.

Helen I think you live in a fantasy world.

Ann I was over there, wasn't I? Macrobiotics and truth-games and the politics of Karma or something, she'd be better off with the Moonies. Meister made me sit cross-legged for five minutes staring into his eyes while he held my hands and stared into mine. I don't know what was supposed to happen, maybe it's a Yoga way of making love; but anyway nothing did, except halfway through I farted ...

Helen picks up her book again and tries to read

I'm surprised you hadn't noticed.

Helen What?

Ann Kate's obsession with her bowels. I thought you therapeutic people had an eye for that kind of thing.

Helen Not off-duty, lovey.

Ann Well, what would you say in the trade? About someone who shits all the time? Give me your diagnosis.

Helen It seems to me you're the anally obsessive one.

Ann Come on, expatiate your knowledge.

Helen One doesn't expatiate knowledge. What a pity you didn't stay on for your O-levels.

Ann Well, whatever you do. Isn't it something to do with gift-giving? "The first gift a child can give is its faeces." Do you think she's asking for love?

Helen Do shut up, Ann.

Ann No, we ought to take her seriously. If she feels she's being ignored she might start bringing it out in polythene bags. Or is it a creative act?

... Maybe they're the same thing, I mean stem from the same need: the desire to give and the desire to create. One talks about someone having a gift. Am I on the right lines ...? The original gift is the mother's milk; which the child pays back in the only way it knows how, in the form of turd. Or later, by a process of sublimation, by creating a work of art, a *symbolic* turd, a turd on a higher plane. Am I getting warm?

Pause

So what do you think? Is she a genius or just mother-fixated?
Helen You're so sharp you'll cut yourself. (*She looks at her watch, then reaches across to the radio and switches it on. It comes on—very loud, pop music*)
Ann You'll disturb Dad!
Helen Sorry. (*She turns it down low*) Where's Radio Four on this thing?
Ann Haven't the foggiest, old fruit. Don't go in for that sort of chat. We're all philistines in Bristol, dontcherknow.
Helen I want to catch the news.
Ann Get a better class of news on Four, do you?

Helen turns the dial until she finds what is probably Radio Four. She turns the volume just loud enough to hear when the news comes on

Ann What do you want to hear the news for on a day like this?
Helen There happens to be a crisis on, haven't you heard?
Ann Nah. Don't know nuffing abaht that. Don't reckon crisises. I mean, s'borin', in it? (*She leans back, appreciating the sun*) Marvellous weather ... God, if thou existeth, ta muchly ... You know what I'd like to do? Sunbathe naked.
Helen A sight for sore eyes that'd be.
Ann Wouldn't it? Like a beached whale ...

Slight pause. Now Ann speaks as if repeating a lesson, over-enunciating, savouring the sounds

Die Sonne scheint. Le soleil brille ... Les oiseaux ... chantent ... Ich trink Wein ... unter das, den, dem ... Himmel ... Je nouris ma, mon ... bèbè ... Tout à coup le monde ... s'arrêt ... Achtung, achtung, kommt ... nun ... die Ende ... des, der ... Welt. (*She makes a popping noise with her finger*)

Helen Maybe it's a good thing you didn't waste time taking O-Levels.
Ann Do we *have* to have that?

Helen takes out the ear-plug, plugs it in—the sound goes off—and puts it in her ear. Ann takes a plum and bites into it. Helen reaches across for one. Ann puts her hand down over them

They're *mine*. I picked them. (*She draws them to her side of the table, and eats her plum with relish*) Mmm ... While you were slaving in the kitchen, aah ... Poor Helen, always left with the washing up while the rest of us are out picking plums and having babies, aah, it's not fair ...

Pause. They look at each other. Ann passes across one of the plums

There you are. A handout for the underprivileged.
Helen Thank you.
Ann What do you do at your place, Helen? Your Wandsworth place?
Helen What do you mean, what do I do?
Ann I've never quite understood whether it's a nuthouse, a dosshouse or a communist cell. Is it a front organisation?
Helen I'm not a Party member any more, you know that.
Ann But you're still a Marxist?
Helen Sort of, I suppose. Theoretically.
Ann What, a free-lance one? Or are you a mole?

No answer

Only I would have thought that from a Marxist point of view it's not a good thing to *cure* your patients' hangups. I mean you don't want them *contented*, do you? (*Slight pause*) Correct me if I'm wrong. The aim of the psychotherapist is to slot people back into society. And the aim of the Marxist is to alienate people from society. And you're both ... So my guess *is*, what you're up to there is churning out politically disaffected nuts. The Paranoid Schizophrenic Workers' Party ... What happens after the revolution? Is psychosis a bourgeois indulgence? Or part of the capitalist plot? Will paranoid schizophrenia wither away?

Slight pause

Helen If you don't want to know about things, why don't you shut up?
Ann But I do want to know (*Pause*). All right, now I want to know. What *do* you do? (*Pause*) Helen?
Helen We stop gaps.
Ann What?
Helen We stop gaps. We help a few people who've fallen down cracks in the system. That's all. Or try to. Try to stop them falling any further ... Save the institutions a bit of money.
Ann You make it sound as if it *is* just a dosshouse. What about the therapy.
Helen We don't call it therapy.
Ann Why not? You used to when you did it with your hubby.
Helen Ex-hubby.
Ann When you did it with your hubby before he was your ex-hubby. Why don't you call it therapy like you did when—?
Helen Because we don't set out to cure people, that's why. It's not therapy most of them need; it's to start again from scratch.
Ann So what do you *do*?
Helen Keep them out of trouble. Try and stop them wrecking the place, setting fire to it, ripping off the contents. Talk to them, let them talk; mostly let them talk.
Ann What do they talk about?

Helen Most of the time they're trying to justify themselves. They assume we're making judgements.
Ann Are you?
Helen Not moral ones.
Ann What kind then?
Helen You can come along and help if you're interested.
Ann What would I do?
Helen Listen to them. Mop up sick. Things like that.
Ann Sounds a gas.
Helen Mm.

Ann eats a plum. Helen adjusts the radio controls, saying almost to herself:

Helen Of course there's a dichotomy. I don't need you to tell me.
Ann A *di-chotomy?*
Helen Ssh!

Helen is attentive to the radio. A slight pause. Ann gives a little movement and puts a hand to her belly. A plane goes over

Ann (*to the baby*) Can you hear that, my love?
Helen Damn ...

Helen puts the volume up, putting a hand over one ear. The plane goes. Ann sings softly to herself. After a while Helen turns the radio off and removes the ear plug. Slight pause

Ann Well? What news of the bold bad world?

Helen doesn't answer

Time to put bags on our heads yet, is it?
Helen Oh, don't be so childish!
Ann You can take it seriously if you like, just don't expect me to.
Helen Maybe you'll have to.
Ann When I have to I will, won't I? Why should I spoil my afternoon? I can't do anything about it, can I? Neither can you. (*She leans her head back to the sun*) Anyway, it's not real. None of it's real. It's a figment of a disordered imagination ...

Pause

Helen Is Terry still in Ireland?
Ann Yes.
Helen When's he coming back?
Ann Some time. It depends how things go.
Helen What things?
Ann The tour. The money.
Helen You mean it's not planned?
Ann It's open-ended. They might go to the north.
Helen They are getting paid for the—gigs, are they?
Ann Well, you know how it is.
Helen No.

Ann The bread isn't their motivation. They're musicians, they're not businessmen.

Helen What's to stop them being both?

Ann They're not made that way. They're just going around playing music.

Helen It's a question of artistic integrity, is it?

Ann Stop needling me.

Helen You can talk ... He is going to be around for the birth, I take it?

Ann If he isn't I can manage on my own, can't I? I wish you'd all stop worrying about me.

Helen It's not you I'm worrying about, it's that in there. It's going to be a human being, you know.

Ann You reckon? Oh, gee!

Helen In spite of what you may think, everything's *not* always for the best. Problems don't always solve themselves. We are decision-making animals. Some animals have claws and teeth. We have the ability to make decisions. That's how we made this world. It's ours, for better or worse, we have to deal with it.

Ann What are you talking about?

Helen Oh, nothing.

Ann You're all dying for me to have problems, aren't you?

Helen You know that's not fair.

Ann You lot see life like a TV documentary. Talking heads. Nothing's real unless it's a *problem*. Or best of all, a *crisis*, lovely. Then you call in the talking heads to *discuss* it. Till the problem dies of boredom.

Helen I'm only saying—

Ann All I'm doing is having a baby and minding my own business. It's been done before, without the help of a panel of experts. You open your legs and out it comes. I don't need experts looking up there.

Helen In a squat with no money.

Ann It's not a squat, it's a short-term tenancy.

Helen I beg your pardon.

Ann We pay rates. It's not a squat. We'd pay rent if they'd take it. And what if it is? As for money, junior here's not opening a bank account for a while, and I don't have to draw out my milk through Natwest ... *You* live in a squat. With a bunch of nuts.

Helen I'm not having a baby.

Ann Go and get sired then, get your own problem!

Pause

Ann reaches for the wine bottle. Empty. She looks up at it for a moment as if making a decision, then gets up and takes it into the house

Helen takes out a packet of cigarettes, takes one out. She thinks for a moment, then puts it back in the packet. She reads

Fox What is for the observer a hiatus, is for them a natural passing of time. They sit in the sun, by the bed, on the lavatory seat, in the kitchen, reading, talking, musing ... The sun which shone on Freud, Marx and Jesus still shines. The same one. On Hannibal, Hitler, Neanderthal man,

Darwin. Kate has come out of the lavatory, washed her hands perfunctorily; pauses by the bedroom door, listening to the murmur of the mother's voice ... Kate lives in—Hamburg. If asked why, she talks of finding her own space, cutting her roots, searching for an autonomous self. We are defined, from birth, by gender, parentage, class, nationality, as such and such. We wear the stereotypes like strait-jackets, become them. Somewhere underneath is the true individual, the true free self ... And so on ... Or will say, why not live in Hamburg? Why do you, not? She works, part-time, in various jobs; one must not define her by her occupation. She has dabbled in her time, or as she would say, got into, TM, *Gestalt*, encounter groups, yoga, the i ching, Zen ...

Kate comes out from the house. She carries a small synthetic paper bag

Kate Here you are.

Helen looks up, registers the bag, and is for a moment bereft of words

Annie said to give it to you. It's a cold sausage. I suppose it's some sort of joke.

Helen Oh, my God, that bloody child ...

Kate I thought so.

Helen starts giggling in spite of herself

What's funny?

Helen Nothing, dear.

Helen returns to her book. Kate shrugs and sits down

Ann enters from the house with a bottle of wine held by the corkscrew, which she has driven into the cork

Ann Ah, wouldn't she accept it?

Kate What?

Ann puts the bottle on the table

Ann Here, I can't get this cork out.

Helen continues reading

I don't want to give myself a miscarriage, do I? Or do I? Would that be a solution to the problem?

Kate Give it here.

Ann Going to do some karate on it?

Kate takes the bottle and tries to remove the cork. Nothing happens. She takes a couple of breaths, closes her eyes, pauses, pulls the cork without effort

Your guru would be proud of you. Slosh it round.

Kate fills three glasses

Kate Anything else I can do for you?

Ann Contemplate your navel, dear, I'll holler when I want you.

Kate sits down, takes a drink. She puts the glass down and stretches, arms above her head, arching her back. Pause

Helen I think it's time we had a talk about Mum.

The others don't answer

She's going to be on her own.

Kate You think one of us ought to stay around?

Helen That's what I want to talk about.

Kate Right.

Slight pause

Helen I know for you two everything sorts itself out in some vague mystic way. Only if it doesn't I shall be the one to cope.

Kate I wasn't thinking of going straight back.

Helen How long can you stay?

Kate A fortnight.

Helen Is that all?

Kate They won't hold the job otherwise.

Helen It's only part-time, isn't it?

Kate It's my *job*, Helen. It's what I live on. I've got commitments too, I'm not a tourist, I live out there.

Helen I'm only asking.

Kate What about you?

Helen I'll stay if necessary, Mum comes first. Only it's difficult leaving the Centre just now.

Kate You need a holiday from that place.

Helen I couldn't agree more.

Kate Can't they manage between them, Bill and what's-her-name?

Helen Nancy? She's useless. She won't be staying much longer.

Kate I thought you said she loved the work.

Helen Oh, she did at first, playing Florence Nightingale. Only she's a romantic, she expected gratitude to go with it, she expected them all to love her. And that you don't get. It's just bloody hard work, and bloody unrewarding. She went to France for a week and brought back a big bottle of Benedictine. Gave everyone a little nip as a treat, put it away in her cupboard, and naturally someone nicked it. "How could they!" she said. "After all I've done!" As if they notice.

Kate You sound as if you hate them.

Helen They can't help themselves, poor buggers. It's their dependence I hate. And the society that's made them like that.

Kate You've been there too long. Why don't you make a change? You've done your bit.

Helen Don't make me sound like a martyr. It's a job, that's all.

Kate Which you hate.

Helen I said it's *difficult*.

Kate And unrewarding.

Helen What about it? Why should one expect rewards?

Ann Saint Helen.

Helen I don't mean it like that.

Kate You're not getting anything *out* of it, are you? You're just adding one more dissatisfied person to the world ...

Helen Oh, don't give me that stuff.

Kate You can't help other people to a full life if you're leading an empty one yourself.

Helen Look, I'm not in the business of producing full lives. I'm trying to help a few people not to turn into institutionalized wrecks, that's all, trying to patch up a little bit of the damage. I'm not an idealist like you and I don't have any theories left and the way things are going nothing's going to matter any more soon anyway. Meanwhile you carry on with your consciousness raising and let me get on with my job.

Kate Don't be catty, dear.

Pause

Helen The Council's trying to get us out, you know, throwing an eviction order at us.

Kate Why?

Helen You tell me. We're saving them money. Maybe they need their consciousness raised. Shall I give you their addresses? (*Pause*) Look at that sky.

Kate What's wrong with it?

Helen The world could be such a good place to live in.

Ann It is.

Pause

Kate Mum may not want us around. She may want to be alone for a while.

Helen She hasn't lived alone since she was married. I don't know how she'll cope.

Kate She won't be the first ... It might give her a chance to find herself.

Helen To do what?

Kate To find out who she is.

Helen Oh, my God ...

Kate What's wrong with that?

Helen Nothing. Nothing.

Ann I'll stay.

Kate and Helen look at Ann

No sweat.

Helen You're having a baby, lovey, have you forgotten?

Ann What about it?

Helen What about it ...

Ann It's not due for three weeks. I could have it here for that matter.

Kate I thought you were booked in at Bristol.

Ann They can't stop me having it here if I want to. Can they?

Kate Annie, you're supposed to have the first one in hospital, in case of complications.

Ann There won't be any complications.

Helen Oh, don't be stupid.

Ann Can they stop me having it here?

Kate They can't *stop* you.

Ann Well then, that's settled. I'll stay here and have it. So now you'll have to find something else to worry about. (*Pause*) I'm going to see Dad.

Ann gets up and goes into the house

Helen I wish she didn't irritate me so much.

Kate You encourage her.

Helen Do I?

Kate It's a game you play, you two. She knows she only has to rub against you. You're the match to her matchbox.

Helen Hm.

Kate Like the way she used to chase you with that smelly bit of chewed wool. The more angry you got the harder she tried to shove it in your face.

Helen It was disgusting.

Kate What's the book?

Helen shows her the cover

Kate "Where Freud Went Wrong." Did he?

Helen It would be nice to think so.

Kate Why?

Helen He took our freedom away, didn't he? I mean our sense of freedom.

Kate He never said we weren't free.

Helen Kate, he spent his life saying it. Everything we do has a cause, a motive, an explanation. Spontaneous actions don't fit into Freud's scheme. You can't have it both ways. Freud would explain exactly why Annie chased me with that bit of stinky wet wool.

Kate Why she chose to.

Helen What's the difference? And why I get angry at her. And why we all believe in the scentific method but can't accept its implications.

Kate You mean we *have* to think we're free.

Helen Yes. Nice paradox, isn't it?

Kate I suppose so. It's all a bit of a wank really, isn't it, whether you're free or only think you're free. What difference does it make to anything?

Helen None, I suppose.

Kate Well then.

Helen Did I ever tell you about my dream? Not really a dream; I suddenly wake up sometimes, on a very dark night, and feel as if I know exactly what it means for the whole thing to be a machine.

Kate What whole thing?

Helen Everything. The universe. Us. No point, no purpose, just a running on till it stops.

Kate What does it matter?

Helen It matters to me when it happens in the middle of the night.
Kate Freud would explain it.
Helen Yes, he would.

Pause

Fox The same sun looks down—though slanting now—which once saw a
dead earth. Saw nothing, of course, just shone. Then on the first primi-
tive forms, as we call them. On through history. Shines now on Kate
and Helen discussing Freud and freedom ... In an hour it'll be down,
the sun, behind the trees. As we say; it doesn't really go down. It goes
round and round ... Relatively speaking.
Helen It's her improvidence I can't stand.
Kate She's got a different attitude from you that's all, don't get so heavy
about it.
Helen She's going to have a baby, for Heaven's sake.
Kate So what? She'll cope. She may make a marvellous mother.
Helen At someone else's expense.
Kate What do you mean?
Helen You know how she operates. Puts on her lilies of the field act and
leaves us to do the worrying.
Kate I don't worry.
Helen Well I do.
Kate That's your problem, isn't it?
Helen And Mum.
Kate So you're worrying about Mum worrying about Annie.
Helen Do you think it's a good idea for her to have it here?
Kate It's not our decision to make, is it?
Helen Mum's bound to say yes ... I'm not even sure she really wants the
kid.
Kate She could have done something about it, couldn't she?
Helen Annie? Do something about something?
Kate Do stop getting at her, Helen.
Helen I do, don't I?
Kate Yes.
Helen Freud would explain it. Papa Freud. All we have to do is do what
we do, Freud will explain it. (*Pause*) I wish he'd go. It's so strange;
waiting for—nothing. Suddenly he's gone. Nothing happens, he just
goes. Forever. No more chances.
Kate It happens to everyone.
Helen Yes, dear.
Kate I mean it's part of the process. Part of the meaning.
Helen I see. And what's the rest of the meaning?
Kate You're a bit low at the moment, aren't you?
Helen What do you expect ...? Did you know him?

Kate looks at her, thinking about it

Kate We never really communicated.
Helen Do you think Mum did? (*Pause*) Do you think he did?

Slight pause

Kate I know what you mean though. The sun ought to go out when someone dies.
Helen It'd be out all the time. (*Slight pause*. *Helen nods towards the radio*) The news doesn't help.
Kate That'll go too.
Helen Maybe.

Pause. Kate looks across at Helen. She dum-dums a few bars of "Hearts and Flowers". Helen smiles

Hey, do you remember those two schoolgirls bicycling along to St Mark's, straw hats on the back of their heads, all bright-eyed and bushy-tailed?
Kate Who?
Helen Us, dear.
Kate My God, we haven't got to the remembering back stage, have we?
Helen I was so full of excitement I used to have to run round and round in the breaks to let off the energy. All those lovely things ahead of us: leaving school; sex . . .
Kate Though not in that order.
Helen Well, no.
Kate And your decadent club.
Helen Oh yes.
Kate Which you wouldn't let me join.
Helen It was secret.
Kate I used to wonder what you did.
Helen Smoked and talked about sex. Though only two of us had had it.
Kate You being one?
Helen No, no, when it happened to me I left. I wasn't going to talk about it to *them*.
Kate And the dirty Noddy jokes we used to tell in the Brownies . . . And Mr Franklin at Sunday School who you had a crush on.
Helen He had bad breath, poor lamb . . . Gentle Jesus meek and mild. Blessed are the meek. Turn the other cheek. All things bright and beautiful. Jesus standing in the doorway with his lamp, looking so kind. Suffer the little children . . . I think of that, and think of the Vietnam photographs . . . I suppose we were meant to believe it . . . Did *they* believe it? I'm sure nice Mr Franklin did; with his foul breath. He'd talk of gentle Jesus, and we'd cower away . . . Maybe that's part of the trouble.
Kate What?
Helen That conditioning. Those awful lies. Dreadful hypocrisies. Damnable . . .

Pause. Kate fiddles idly with the radio

Kate Maybe there really is someone out there listening in.
Helen Gentle Jesus?
Kate No, no. Another civilization.

Helen What, little green people with feelers?
Kate Why not big golden people?
Helen I didn't know you were one of *those* as well.
Kate One of what?
Helen Those Close Encounters people. Sci-fi Adventists. So you think they might suddenly come down out of the sky and put it all right?
Kate Oh, *I* don't know ... Fucking hell ...

Helen looks across at her, but Kate says nothing

Helen Do you want some plums?
Kate Mm, great.

Helen gets up and exits to the end of the garden

Kate watches her go. Then she gets up, to lie on her back on the grass, eyes closed, relaxed. Pause

Fox The trick is to bring body and mind into harmony. Most important is relaxation. Not the Western form, the flopping exhausted into a stuffed chair to goggle at the telly. No, this is creative, one might say active relaxation of psyche and soma, a letting go while holding on. Kate has worked at this. "Worked at it", of course, is the wrong term; one must work at not working at it. She found it difficult, the paradox bothered her, of pushing and letting go at the same time. "Think of a good bowel action" somebody once told her. She found a sentence to express it, it seemed as if it might mean something. "Let it push." She repeats it to herself. "Let it push" ... This is called "the corpse position."

Mary comes out from the house. She stands by the table looking down at Kate, then looks out, perhaps at the garden. She is still for a moment. She begins to go back to the house

Kate Mum ...?

Mary comes back as Kate gets up

Mary I thought you were asleep. Where's Helen?
Kate Down the garden. She'll be back in a minute.

Mary sits down. Kate stands for a moment. Then she picks up the bottle

D'you want some wine?
Mary I came out to see if you wanted tea ... Yes, that would be nice.

Kate pours her some, not particular which glass she uses; and some more for herself, sitting down meanwhile

Kate There you are.
Mary Thank you, darling.
Kate Is he asleep?
Mary He is now ... Ann's sitting with him.

Kate is attentive to her mother's mood, but Mary shows nothing

What a lovely day it's been. So unexpected.

Kate Gorgeous.

Mary It's good having you all here. I don't know when was the last time.

Kate Easter.

Mary Was it?

Kate The barbecue.

Mary Oh yes.

Pause

Kate We thought perhaps one of us could stay on for a few weeks. What do you think?

Mary Yes, that would be nice.

Kate Is that what you'd like?

Mary You know I'm always glad to have any of you here.

Kate Mum, that's not what I'm asking. Will you want one of us around?

Mary I can manage.

Kate What about the business side of it? Papers and things.

Mary Oh, that's all taken care of ... You remember John Parrish?

Kate Of course I remember him. Didn't he go and live in the country?

Mary Apparently he didn't like the isolation. He's back anyway. He's got a flat somewhere. Putney.

Kate Has he been there long?

Mary A year or so I think.

Kate He must be getting on a bit.

Mary He's retired.

Kate Have you seen him?

Mary No, no. He wrote when he heard about George, so I rang him up. And he's offered to look after things for me.

Kate Is he on his own?

Mary Yes, I think so.

Slight pause

Kate So that's all taken care of.

Mary Yes ... You know of course there was a spot of bother.

Kate giggles

Kate Oh, Mum ...

Mary What?

Kate "A spot of bother".

Mary Whatever you'd call it ... The grass needs cutting.

Kate I'll do it tomorrow.

Mary No, we have to leave it. The noise ... I didn't tell your father he's been in touch.

Kate Would it bother him?

Mary I've no idea. Anyway, there's no point in bringing it up now ... Not that he'd hear, probably ...

Kate Can I ask something about that business?

Mary Yes, of course.

Kate Did it start after Dad left or before?
Mary Oh, after. That's what brought him back so quickly.
Kate What?
Mary He couldn't stand it.
Kate That you'd got someone else? After he'd left?
Mary Yes.
Kate Christ Almighty. So why did he leave in the first place?
Mary He wanted something he wasn't getting.
Kate What?
Mary I don't know. He said freedom but that wasn't it. He'd have come
back anyway, I think. He couldn't help himself. He was a very intense
man. He cried.
Kate Do you mind talking about it?
Mary No. It's like talking about somebody else; or something I read ...
I didn't make any decisions, you see. Things happened around me,
happened to me, and I—watched it happen. Even the emotional part—
I just happened to be the one it was happening to.
Kate Oh, Mum ...
Mary Mm ...
Kate So Parrish just—(*She makes a flitting movement with her hand*) Was
that how you wanted it?
Mary I don't remember.
Kate You just let it all happen?
Mary Who was I to stop it ... Anyway, water over the mill.
Kate Under.
Mary Yes, I suppose it would be.

Pause

Kate How are you?
Mary I'm fine. A bit tired.
Kate You should have got a nurse in full-time. Why didn't you?
Mary Oh, there was no need for that. There's nothing much to do.
Kate It would have given you time off.
Mary I can't take time off, darling.

Pause

Kate It's something I can't imagine: being stuck with the same person all
your life.
Mary Stuck with?
Kate You know what I mean. All the allowances you must have to make;
all the compromises. How do you hang on to *yourself*? I mean how do
you separate what you want from what's best or—expedient? Or does it
all become the same thing?
Mary You've lived with people.
Kate Never for long ... That's why I went to Germany. To try and sort
that out. You remember the state I was in.
Mary I thought it was very brave of you.
Kate It felt more like a cop-out at the time. I had to go. I was too tangled

up here, I couldn't separate myself out, you know? Culture, family, David, all pulling at me from outside. And a real me somewhere inside it all ... Sitting in that God-awful room in Hamburg, not knowing a soul; sending you cheery letters and feeling suicidal; well, bloody. Missing David like mad. Missing everything. Trying to work out what it meant to be free to be me. (*She laughs it down*) If anything. Thinking, what the hell is it all about? Does it have to be a choice between running away from love and losing your freedom? You don't really know what I'm on about, do you?

Mary I don't think we thought a great deal about freedom in my day; I mean personal freedom.

Kate So you never felt that love was a—limiting thing?

Mary Oh, well, once, perhaps. When Helen came along.

Kate Did you plan us?

Mary Not exactly.

Kate This has to mean no.

Mary We didn't plan not to have you. I mean we took precautions but we—didn't worry all that much.

Kate Accidental on purpose.

Mary That's about it ... When I had Helen I got the most incredible maternal feelings. Like a love affair. I felt trapped in it. Taken over by some intense thing which *I* hadn't asked for, which had nothing to do with me. Trapped. Part of me felt it was all wrong, I'd been put upon. Only there was no way of expressing it then, nobody seemed to understand. Least of all me. I told myself not to be stupid. "Don't you want the child?" "Yes." And from somewhere inside: "No, no, no!"

Kate So what happened?

Mary Oh, it's very easy to fall into being a mother. And a good thing too, I suppose.

Kate And then you had me, and then you had Annie ...

Mary Mmm.

Slight pause

Kate Did I tell you I've got a new bloke?

Mary No.

Kate Not at all what you'd expect. Very straight. He wants to get married ... He's forty-seven. Divorced. He's got some money ... He's very nice. Quite ordinary really ... What are you going to do?

Mary looks across the garden, not answering

Helen reappears

Helen It's like a jungle down there ... The wasps are having a great time ... How is he?

Mary The same ... Annie's singing to him.

Kate Captive audience.

Pause

Helen She wants to stay here.

Mary Hm?

Helen She wants to have her kid here. That's what she says. I expect she'll change her mind. I thought you ought to know, in case she suddenly springs it on you.

Mary What about what's-his-name, Terry?

Helen I don't know. Perhaps he assumes he's done his job. Anyway, it's out of the question, isn't it?

Kate Not necessarily.

Helen Oh, you know what'll happen. Mum'll find herself having to look after it. Saddled with it.

Kate Only if she wants to be. She can make up her own mind, can't you, Mum?

Helen Don't be naïve. You know how these things work.

Kate I wish you wouldn't try and boss people around all the time. Mum can take care of herself. And you don't have to always expect the worst of Annie.

Helen I don't expect the worst of her; I just expect her to stay in character. What has she ever given her mind to for any length of time? She can't even finish a book. Maybe she'll metamorphose into a responsible mother, but I wouldn't bank on it. And I don't think Mum should. It's too risky. She's done her stint of bringing up kids. Haven't you, Mum?

Mary I quite like the idea of being a gran.

Helen Not on the premises, Mum. It won't work.

Kate You don't know it won't. Anyway, it's not our business.

Helen Well, it's up to you ... Apart from the possibility of Terry bringing his band down ... Camping out in the garden ...

Kate You've made your point, Helen.

Pause

Fox A cloud, we may imagine, passes over the sun. For a moment; it'll go. The forecast is rain for tomorrow. But then, the forecast was rain for today. Upstairs Annie sings softly. If she were told her father is past hearing, she'd say, perhaps he hears, somehow. And anyway, why shouldn't I sing? I feel like singing. I like singing. Let me sing ... The father was a business man of some sort. As a lad, he had a burning desire to work in the pits at a motor racetrack. But it was decided against. A fairly successful business man; he leaves some money ... Other mistakes are made, apart from the weather. Prognostications go awry. Human error, technical error; computor error. The factor left out, as factors are. Perhaps a touch of deathwish somewhere, the Valhalla complex. Perhaps more than a touch of simple built-in viciousness, kept under, having to express itself at last ... So that, somewhere, at this moment, we may imagine, men sit in shirtsleeves, staring at screens, picking up phones, grey, yellow, red, talking technicalese, acting their parts; shirts darkened under the armpits. It could sort itself out, it has before.

Kate You could do with a bit of Annie in you.

Helen looks at Kate

A touch of what you call improvidence. Which is a trust in providence.

Helen You mean God? And when you find he's out for the day, other people?

Kate Yes, trust in people. Trust in events; trust in the present.

Helen The present's all right, it's the future bothers me.

Kate That's what I mean. You spend all your time worrying about the future.

Helen I don't spend all my time—

Kate You're not responsible for the world carrying on. You're not Atlas. Loosen off and enjoy yourself.

Helen I do, what are you talking about?

Kate You hold the reins too tight.

Helen What's that from, some book?

Kate It is as a matter of fact. The novice rider holds on too tight. His mind and body live in the future, taking action against what might happen, fighting phantoms. Only when he learns to trust the future does he come back into the present. He relaxes, goes with the horse instead of trying to drive it.

Helen And if the horse wants to go the wrong way?

Kate There is no wrong way.

Helen Oh, come off it.

Kate He puts it right as it happens. He doesn't think about it.

Helen Reflex action.

Kate That's your trouble, you don't trust your reflexes.

Helen I don't trust the world's reflexes. Right, what about a lecture on Zen archery now.

Kate It's the same thing. Training the reflexes. That's all yoga does; teaches you to trust that part of you that *knows*, without you having to tell it all the time.

Helen Is it true you've got a guru?

Kate Did Annie tell you that?

Helen Meister.

Kate Herman. He's a joke. He eats nothing but brown rice. He was quite interesting at first, then he got boring. Well, they've all got a bit boring. As if they've stuck, you know?

Helen She said at least she's got past self-improvement.

Kate Obviously.

Helen That's what I said.

Mary She's such an intelligent girl.

Helen I think she's brilliant. Such a waste.

Kate Waste of what? She's Annie, what more do you want?

Helen Of her potential.

Kate I suppose if she'd become a nuclear physicist she'd be a fuller person.

Helen By the look of her she's as full as she can get.

Kate It's not what people do that matters, it's what they are.

Helen Rubbish ...

Kate I'm not going to argue. (*She picks up Helen's book and begins to read*

Helen Anyway, what *is* she? (*Pause*) Poor Mum. Having to put up with squabbling brats ... It's not that I *worry* about the future, it's ... Well, yes it is ... Actually I envy Annie sometimes ... Or would, if I believed it.

Mary Believed what?

Helen Her attitude. I suspect she's putting it on.

Mary One thing she has been is consistent.

Helen That's a fact. She did drop out from nursery school.

Mary No, she didn't take to nursery school.

Helen And wandered back home. And didn't take to school, and didn't take to any of the jobs she had.

Kate (*from her book*) Maybe she found something more important.

Helen And here she is again ... Found *what* more important?

No answer

Sex.

Kate Well? Wouldn't you say human relationships are more important than those boring old jobs she had?

Helen They were only boring jobs because she didn't bother to get any qualifications.

Kate My God! And I thought you were a radical! So you *like* the idea of locking kids up in school just so they can brandish bits of paper about to say they've learnt a lot of irrelevant facts?

Helen I don't like it, it's the way things are.

Kate So they can get a job to get a pension for their boring old age.

Helen You ought to stand for Parliament, dear.

Kate Boring old age because they use up all their potential getting there, and I mean *real* potential. Not potential on the labour market. I remember when you were on about deschooling society and giving everyone Illich to read and here was your sister *doing* it, but of course it's not for doing it's for talking about.

Helen Oh, balls. Do you really think she knew what she was doing?

Kate Of course she didn't. It was a gut reaction. It was real to her. Whereas, of course, the right thing to do is go through the system and then write a thesis on how bad it is.

Pause

Helen Well, you've got a point. All the same ...

Kate Anyway, you're so inconsistent. You go on about how we're not in charge of our own behaviour, you've nothing but sympathy for those smelly dropouts you look after, but when it comes to your own sister you haven't got a good word for her. Charity begins at home, dear.

Pause

Helen Freud would explain it.

Kate I don't agree with the way she lives if you want to know, I don't think she can live that way and not come a cropper as things are. But at least she's being honest with herself.

Helen I don't think she is, you see ...

Pause

Kate We shouldn't argue.

Helen And when she does come a cropper she's going to have a kid with her. Will you be willing to give up that freedom you're so keen on, to help bale her out? (*Slight pause*) Self-expression can be an indulgence.

Mary I don't see why she shouldn't cope perfectly well.

Helen Yes, I daresay she will. Don't take any notice of us, Mum, it's all hot air. We get carried away by our own verbosity, don't we squirt?

Kate (*reading*) "In attempting to reassert as a basic truth that the individual is both unique and free. I make no apology for using terms such as 'morality', 'virtue', even 'soul'."

Helen He's a Catholic.

Kate Oh, that explains it. He's got to believe in personal freedom, otherwise poor old God couldn't judge us ... Fancy sending someone to hell and it was really because he had a deprived childhood ... Maybe they've given St Peter and that lot the push and got in a team of consultant psychiatrists ... No more hell, we all go to purgatory for analysis ... The rehabilitation centre in the sky ...

Pause

Mary My mother was convinced she'd go straight to Heaven.

Kate Did she say so?

Mary More or less. She just didn't see why she shouldn't.

Kate Why, was she so good?

Mary No, but she had a nice nature and never needed to be bad. I mean she got everything she wanted.

Helen What a lovely way to go.

Mary Yes. It seems unfair somehow.

Kate I remember her. She was round and red like an apple, wasn't she? A crinkly apple, like the ones she had on her sideboard.

Helen Did she have a good life?

Mary She was the only really happy person I've ever known.

Helen And didn't mind dying?

Mary No. She looked forward to it when the time came.

Helen Incredible.

Mary She married at seventeen. Not exactly an arranged marriage, but it was taken for granted even when she was still at school. I think he was a second cousin. They married in nineteen-fifteen. He was due to go to France so they decided to get married first. The story goes that he had a stag party with his mates. They were larking about in the road and a Hansom cab went over his foot. So he never got to France.

Kate The story goes? Do you mean he did it on purpose?

Mary I've no idea.

Kate We may all owe our existence to that Hansom cab.

Kate Well done Grandad.

Helen And they lived happily every after.

Mary Yes, more or less. They lived all their lives in the same house. They had six children.

Kate And she never ... I mean ...
Mary What?
Kate I don't know.
Mary Things were different then.
Kate Expectations were lower.
Helen What do you mean, expectations? What more could she expect?

Pause

Kate Would you say Dad's had a good life?

Slight pause

Mary I don't know, darling. It depends what you mean, I suppose. (*Pause. She gets up*) I'd better go and rescue him from Annie's singing.
Kate Let me take over.
Mary No, I'll go.
Kate Let me, you sit here.
Mary It's not a question of taking over. I want to.

Mary goes into the house

Helen What did you have to say that for?
Kate What?
Helen Did he have a good life.
Kate What's wrong with that?
Helen You've upset her, haven't you?
Kate I don't think so.
Helen She's doing her best to hold herself together. Don't make it more difficult for her.
Kate It doesn't help to pussyfoot around. If she's got something inside it's best for it to come out.
Helen It doesn't help to go galumphing through private lives like an elephant either.
Kate What are you talking about? Stop over-reacting.
Helen Not everyone wants to live out your theories. Some things are private.

Slight pause

Kate Seems to me you're the one who's upset.

Pause

Helen You're right. I over-reacted.
Kate Why was that?
Helen Freud would know.
Kate Did he, do you think? Have a good life?
Helen Dad? He kept himself together.
Kate Not saying much, is it?
Helen I think it's saying quite a lot.
Kate For one of your nuts perhaps. He kept himself together by not using himself; shutting himself in.
Helen He was a good father ... And he did have his fling, didn't he?

Kate And came back.
Helen It was his decision. There's a romantic idea that when something like that happens it's necessarily a Good Thing, expressing one's true self. But coming back was his decision too. Maybe that was the Good Thing. Maybe a shut-in person expresses himself best by being shut-in.
Kate I can't believe that. I find it—defeatist. By the way—John Parrish is back in town.
Helen Really?
Kate He's acting as sort of executor. Dealing with the papers and stuff.
Helen Ah ... Well, that's good.
Kate Dad doesn't know, by the way.
Helen What are you trying to tell me?
Kate I've told you. Parrish got in touch, and he's ...
Helen He got in touch?
Kate Mum wouldn't, would she?
Helen Is he—attached to anyone?
Kate Apparently not.
Helen Hm.
Kate Exactly.
Helen Exactly what?

Kate shrugs

Perhaps we shouldn't be talking like this.
Kate I'm only giving you the news.
Helen You're not. You're thinking what I'm thinking. (*Pause*) She could do a lot worse.
Kate She *what*?
Helen After a decent interval ... Couldn't she?
Kate You're joking.
Helen Why not?
Kate Oh my Christ ...
Helen Will you kindly explain yourself? He's all right, he's a nice guy.
Kate I'm not saying he's not. He's a lovely guy. I'm sure he'd do a great job. He'd protect her and cherish her.
Helen Then what the fuck are you on about?
Kate Helen, my love, I will not have Mum shacking up with a nice guy! A nice guy is the last thing she'll want.
Helen Oh, rubbish.

Ann approaches

Kate Ssh ... *Pas devant l'enfant.*

Ann looks at them both, and sits down. She pours some wine

Helen You shouldn't drink so much.
Ann What were you talking about?
Kate You'll have an alcoholic baby.
Ann Good luck to him.
Helen Him?

Ann He, she or it.

Kate You know how parents book up for Eton? You'd better book yours a place in Skid Row.

Ann What were you talking about?

Helen Grownup talk, my dear. So what did you give him, your popular medley?

Kate Or was it *The Nuns' Chorus*?

Ann What are you on about?

Helen We heard you were singing to him.

Ann What if I was? You two can be so childish. (*Pause*) He recognised me. He opened his eyes.

(*Pause*)

Helen What about your antenatals?

Ann My what?

Helen Don't tell me you haven't been going.

Ann Oh, those.

Helen You'll regret it. They make it easier.

Ann I don't want it easier. I want a child born of agony. I want it to enter on a scream.

Helen You should have been an actress.

Kate Seriously, you should go to antenatals.

Ann Why? People never used to.

Helen People never used to eat cornflakes, do you want to give them up?

Ann Look, people have always had babies, it's a natural thing to do. I'm not going to treat it as if it's some kind of illness. I'm expecting a child, not an ulcer.

Kate You've got the wrong idea, Annie. Those exercises are to *make* it more natural.

Ann *More natural*. What does that mean?

Kate It means we don't live in a natural world any more, we don't live naturally. Women don't squat for one thing, we've given up squatting ...

Helen She hasn't.

Kate We sit on chairs, that's not natural. We don't use our bodies naturally any more, we just carry them about.

Ann Women used to just have babies.

Kate Yes, and they used to use their bodies, they worked their bodies.

Helen They didn't just loaf around all the time.

Ann I don't loaf around ... I wish you'd all leave me alone. (*Pause*) You complicate everything ... Dirty everything up.

Kate We don't even know how to breathe properly any more. We've lost our bodies.

Ann Speak for yourself. I've got two now. (*Slight pause*) I helped get the lunch, didn't I? Who made the bean salad? (*Pause*) I don't understand dying.

Kate You're not supposed to. You're too young. There's a time to live and a time to die. Ripeness is all. You're not ripe yet, young Annie.

Ann I feel pretty ripe.
Kate What, that? That's just a precocious podding.
Ann Podding, I like that. I'm in pod. I'm in the podding club ... You
know that pink thing climbing up the wall? I was looking at it and
suddenly one of the pods went ping, and seeds shot everywhere.
Imagine having babies like that. Human grapeshot. Midwives standing
like fielders, waiting for a catch.
Helen Nothing's sacred for the younger generation any more.
Ann Bollocks.
Kate Mocking childbirth. Dropping litters out of wedlock. Taking the
name of bollocks in vain.
Ann Bollocks. Everything's sacred to me ... Do you know there's a sign
outside the antenatal clinic saying 'Drop no litter'?
Helen You did go then?
Ann I went four weeks running (*She turns her face to the sun*) *Die Sonne
Scheint ... Les oiseaux ... chantent ... Je nourris ma, mon, bèbè ... sous
le soleil ...* (*She puts a hand on her belly*) She had us doing relaxation
exercises. There we lay, two dozen beached whales. "Now, mothers, I
want you all utterly relaxed. Start at the top of your head, and down to
your tiptoes. Let mother earth take charge, you can't fall off. Relax
those buttock muscles, mothers." We dutifully unclenched our bums.
"Now relax your minds, mothers, minds have muscles too. Think beau-
tiful thoughts. Think of a beautiful island in a calm, beautiful sea ..."
I thought of two dozen Etnas, waiting to erupt, learning how to erupt.
My baby kicked, as if to say, "We know, don't we?" I smiled. "Relax
that mouth, mother."
Helen I don't think it would be a good idea for you to have it here, Annie.
Ann *You* don't think?
Helen Mum'll have enough on her plate.
Ann What on her plate? She won't have anything on her plate. Her plate'll
be empty, won't it?
Helen She's got to find a new life for herself.
Ann Got to?
Helen And I don't mean resident nanny.
Ann You are a cow, Helen ... Well I've decided to have it here and that's
that.
Kate What about Terry?
Ann What about him? He's done his job, hasn't he?
Kate Are you joking?

No answer

Has there been any trouble with Terry?
Ann Fathers aren't necessary. Quite efficient mechanisms for impregnation
of ova. All the rest is propaganda by the establishment. To keep the
family together, so that father has a hot supper waiting, to stoke him
up for work.
Helen Is that what Terry said?
Ann There's no trouble. No sweat ... I'm having it here.

Helen You are scared, aren't you?

Ann Bollocks. (*Pause*) It's time you worried about yourself for a change.

Helen What does that mean?

Ann I wouldn't say your life is exactly ...

Kate Leave it off, Annie. Don't start, you two.

Helen Exactly what?

Slight pause

Ann On an even *keel* ... Well, perhaps it is; only the keel's stuck in the mud.

Ann waits. Helen doesn't bite

Physician, heal thyself. (*Pause*) You think I'm a dropout. What are you then? Dropout Marxist ... Dropout therapist ... Dropout wife ... At least I'm having a kid, and I can prove it. Let's see what you've ever done in your life! Give us a run-down! What have you accomplished?!

Kate Dad is dying!

Kate regrets saying it. She stands up, stares at them. Then she goes into the house

CURTAIN

ACT II

Fox Mary, by the bed, looks at her husband's face. His eyes are closed. She watches his breathing, waiting for it to stop. Now and then it does, for a moment. When it does, she waits for it to start again. She finds that looking for long at his face, it becomes the face of a stranger. She looks away, back again. Still a stranger. No, no revelation—It's happened before. She sits by the stranger's bed or rather *her* bed in which lies a stranger. She takes a sip of water, from the bedside table ... He had, we may imagine, only two memories of his very early childhood. One is of his mother—he assumed it must have been—expressing milk from her breasts. The other is of sitting in a tin bath with a yellow celluloid duck.·He doesn't know why he's remembered these two memories of all possible ones. The breasts, of course, are easier than the duck. He's never told anyone of them ... Kate is hanging about, at the foot of the stairs. She went to the house not to go in, but because her body needed to move. She's angry, she has, as she would have said a few years earlier, bad vibes. She's afraid of communicating them to the father. All of the apparently fragmentary universe is in fact a unity. The unifying factor, and at the same time part of the unity—though "part" is the wrong term—is the all-encompassing self. So she's learnt, and believes sometimes, partly. So she hangs about at the foot of the stairs, not wanting her vibes to impinge on a dying. Goes into the kitchen to find another bottle of wine; but there isn't any.

Helen Could we call a truce do you think?

Ann Sure thing big Sis ... Sorry. It's only because you keep getting at me.

Helen I know ... And because you're not so sure of yourself as you pretend to be.

Ann says nothing

We tried for a kid, you know, Tim and I; in the early days.

Ann I didn't know that.

Helen I suppose it's lucky we didn't manage it.

Ann It might have kept you together.

Helen That's what I mean. God forbid.

Ann Why couldn't you?

Helen I don't know, we didn't get around to finding out. By that time the relationship had started to—well, its keel got stuck in the mud, as you put it so delightfully. You ought to write, you've got a nice turn of phrase.

Ann Maybe it was him.

Helen No, he's had one since. With this Norwegian actress, or whatever she is.

Ann Are you still in touch?

Helen Oh, he writes now and then. To say how marvellous everything is.

How happy he is. Now.

Ann Is he still—therapising?

Helen No, no. He's in her father's business. He sells teak furniture. And she's given up her career to be a proper wife and mother for when he comes home to their lovely timber house in the country and to cook him lovely Norwegian things and to look after him and never to argue.

Ann Is that what he told you?

Helen Not exactly. It's the kind of thing he always wanted really, under all that political commitment and social concern. He wanted another mother, only better than the first two.

Ann Two?

Helen I was the second. And now he's got her. And good luck to him.

Ann You mean bad luck to him.

Helen I expect I do ... Maybe it's all anyone wants really, including me, underneath the fine words a cosy childhood that goes on forever. To be wrapped in the mother's arms, warm and fed and safe.

Ann Doesn't sound like your style.

Helen Don't be fooled by style, child. It's just a front.

Ann And underneath the pleasure-principle screaming to get out.

Helen Screaming for its mother.

Ann Do you hate him?

Helen In my profession one's not allowed to hate.

Ann Underneath.

Helen If I knew what was underneath it would be on top, wouldn't it?

Ann You're evading the question.

Helen Why should I hate him?

Ann For leaving you?

Helen He didn't leave me. I kicked him out.

Ann Literally?

Helen Near enough. Threw him out and changed the locks.

Ann Did he try to come back?

Helen Oh yes. He was quite prepared to start again. Or carry on where we left off. Work it through, as he put it. He wrote long letters. He said with our training and experience we ought at least to be able to get our *own* relationship together, or what was the point? I suppose he was right. It was rather ludicrous. You know we used to run a group together. A sort of family structure, we played mother and father. He was very good at it actually. He knew just the right time to get someone angry or upset, and out would come all the bile and resentment. Then we'd examine it together, why they hated their spouses, why they couldn't make relationships. Then home we'd go and get out the knives ... After I kicked him out I wondered if he'd turn up for the group, but he didn't. It could have been quite interesting. To say to them: Well, we've split. Your symbolic Mummy and Daddy have fucked it. Would you like to help *us*?

Ann What did you tell them?

Helen That he was ill. Then that I was ill ... Physician, heal thyself ... (*Pause*) Then he took to telephoning, because I didn't answer the letters. He'd plead, cry. I got an ex-directory number.

Ann Do you miss him?
Helen That bastard?
Ann So what's up?
Helen Who said anything's up?
Ann Come off it, Helen.
Helen A slight loss of confidence, that's all. Probably temporary. Not important.
Ann In yourself?
Helen I had a letter the other day. He's having another kid. Everything's hunky-dory. It's not the best possible thing for one's self-esteem.
Ann Maybe he's putting on a front. He may be miserable.
Helen Is that what I should hope for?
Ann Anyway, you can't blame yourself for not being the right mother for him.
Helen Why not? I picked him. He was obvious enough. I knew what I was walking into. I could see the little brat peeping out from behind the Langian Marxist, mouth puckering up in case he didn't get his ration of love and attention. But that was the late sixties, early seventies. You wouldn't remember.
Ann I've heard rumours.
Helen Yes. Those were the days, my friend . . .
Ann Here we go.
Helen Lots of energy about then. And lots of hope; I suppose they go together. We thought nothing was impossible. I mean we thought everything was curable; given the right treatment; which we were working on. Invention time, game-playing time. *Concerned fun;* that's what we were into. Tim and I played games together. Played politics, played therapy, played marriage. Trying to alter the rules of the game to make it work better. We knew it would be a hard slog, but we had energy on our side, energy and hope.
Ann Were you that ingenuous?
Helen Oh yes. The world was full of Billy Grahams, jolly prophets sweaty with enthusiasm. We didn't believe in original sin, you see, or Freud's thing, the built-in design fault. Society *wasn't* naturally bad—just delinquent. We'd get it playing a different kind of game, one that was more fun, more fulfilling. The creation game instead of the destruction game, giving instead of taking, love instead of war. We looked towards a redemption of Society, a redemption of the individual. A change of the world's heart . . . We did.

Pause

Ann So that's what it is. Poor Helen. Your famous sixties didn't work, did they? Aaah . . . Pushing forty and a life wasted.
Helen Does it sound like self-pity?
Ann Somewhat.
Helen Hm . . . I daresay you're right.
Ann Oh, don't agree with me, Helen!
Helen What's the matter?

Ann (*pleadingly*) Don't agree with me ... I hate it when I win.

Helen What a strange child you are ... Of course there's self-pity in it; resentment. Not only personal though. I mean—I feel I've failed, I mean I've been neither particularly useful nor particularly happy, that must be failure. I know that's a small thing. But I can't separate that failure from the society I was working in. Working for. You can't separate. We are members one of another, as they say ... After Tim went I stopped for a rest. I looked back, I tried to make an honest assessment of where I'd come to, where the world had come to. As if I'd been stuck in the trenches for years, fighting in the trenches, all I knew about the war was my little pocket of it. For the rest, all I had was maps, and books, and theories, and ideals, and hope. And then to be transported to the top of a hill like a general, to see what had really been going on, how the war was really going. I felt very clear-sighted after all that close combat.

Ann And what did you see, O Sage?

Helen Machinery. Events moving as they had to, people behaving as they had to ...

Ann Marx and Freud. I thought that was your *bag*.

Helen Yes. Clever girl. Patterns of inevitability. This is the way things happen, this is why they happened thus ... Yes, I knew that. What I realised was what an intellectual cheat I'd been. We all are. We'll never admit there's anything that can't be explained. Every effect has a cause, every cause has an effect. We don't believe in magic. So when we look at history, or look at ourselves, we see how it had to be like that. But then we say: "Ah, *there's* where it could have been different; just there." And we look more closely; and the hole closes up. Because what we were looking for was action without cause, and you might as well look for perpetual motion. So to get our sense of freedom back we put it into the future. We say: "Oh, yes, it all had to be like that. But from now on, somehow, it's going to be different. From now on ..."

Ann Philosophical masturbation.

Helen All right, this is what I saw from my hilltop: A world that wasn't redeeming itself and never had been. Things getting worse rather than better. I mean there's probably more starvation in the world than there ever was, more deprivation, more brutality; more hypocrisy, more double-thinking, double-dealing, self-serving, time-serving, more inequality, more fat people, more thin people, more homelessness, more cruelty, to animals, to children, to whatever's available; more callousness, more greed, more apathy, more despair ...

Ann There are more of us.

Helen Yes.

Ann Well then.

Helen Well then what? (*Pause*) And looking down close by my hill— You've got the picture, have you? History stretching to the horizon, battlefield after battlefield, and down there close, *my* trenches, where I crouch with my mates, knee-deep in mud and shit, poring over old maps, new maps, constructing theories, on how it's all going and how it can be different. Getting all excited now and then over some new idea: "Let's dig a tunnel and blow them all to blazes. Let's go out and talk to them, get them to understand. Let's educate them, let's politicise them, let's analyse them ..." Me at work: taking in broken people like rejects off the assembly line, patching them up a bit, convincing them it's not so bad out there, they can make it; shoving them out to carry on surviving; our success stories. Not stopping to wonder if survival's enough, it it might be better for rejects to be smashed. And for every one there's another, we don't even keep pace. Fighting a machine, not even fighting, clearing up the mess made by a faulty machine that spews out twisted up people as a by-product. Sweepers-up on the factory floor ... Move to another hill a bit farther off for a better perspective, and it looks much the same, only my trenches now have disappeared, merged with the rest of the battlefield ... So you see, squit, my self-pity isn't only for myself. It's like the love of God; it covers the face of the earth and knows no distinctions.

Pause

Ann Have you done?
Helen Do you want some more?
Ann No thanks ... You *are* a renegade, aren't you? If I were a Marxist I'd crucify you.
Helen Or a Freudian ... Or a Christian. I've cottoned on to their trick, you see, discovered their secret. How they keep themselves sane and raring to go? Whatever they don't like, in people or in societies, they call it a deviation. From the true path; the norm; the predestined way. Look back into history and it's not all that obvious why that particular path should be called the norm and the others deviations, in fact it looks more the opposite. But that's how the story goes- ... A word of advice, my child. Never look back down history.
Ann Gives you vertigo, does it?
Helen Yes. It makes me—sick in my stomach. (*She smiles*)

Pause

Ann A bit *passé*, don't you think, dear? Despair? A bit Jean-Paul Sartre?
Helen I know it's been said before.
Ann I mean literary. You can make words do anything.
Helen So it's not real.
Ann You're making it real. You're making the words make it real.
Helen So if I shut up it'll go away.
Ann I don't mean that. I mean other things are real too, at the same time. Words take over. I don't trust ways of looking at things that pretend that's all there is.
Helen Is that what I'm doing?
Ann You say look how awful everything is. Well, I'm looking. I see a nice garden, I see the sun shining, I feel the sun and it's nice, I've got a baby inside me, when it kicks it makes me laugh ...
Helen So you can ignore all the rest.
Ann *No.* I don't want to *ignore* anything. I know there are awful things.

There's this as well, that's all I'm saying. Why should I ignore this? It's all part of it.

Helen Part of the rich fabric of life.

Ann Right on, man. Count your blessings. Or putting it another way— imagine Sartre reading *La Nausèe* at you—while you're in the middle of a good fuck.

Helen You're too smart for your breeches. (*Pause*) And when the atomic war comes? While you're in the middle of a good fuck?

Ann When?

Helen I fear so.

Ann I don't reckon the future. I dwell in the eternal now. *Jetzt-ist-alles* ... Is that what's bugging you? The bomb?

Helen I suppose so. Finally ... There's always been a redeeming factor. Things might change, they might get better. But *that* ... it's like finals at university. No more pretending you'll do better next term. It'll be the big F for us, as far as I'm concerned. Apparently the idea now is that we can preserve a kind of national nucleus—including, of course, a high proportion of our rulers—to get things going again. They can count me out. There comes a time when you stop making excuses.

Ann Look on the bright side. You'd be able to tell yourself things can't get any worse. (*Pause*) I'm not knocking you, you know ... If you feel like that. And not just putting it on. You may be in the pit of despair for all I know. And you may be right. Only I'm not, you see. I like life, it turns me on. And we are all members one of another. So where does that get us?

Helen Christ knows.

Ann You reckon? (*Pause. She points at the sun*) Look. There's a hydrogen bomb. Isn't it beautiful?

Helen Facile child.

Ann I thought of calling it Solon.

Helen What?

Ann If it's a boy.

Helen *Solon?*

Ann Mm. Do you like it?

Helen What the hell does it mean?

Ann He was a wise old Greek. He was a sage.

Helen It's your child.

Ann Solly. Sol. The sage who knows his onions ... And if it's a girl, Solaria ... And if it's neither ... Neutron.

Helen Won't Terry have a say?

Ann (*absently*) Mmm ...

Helen I'd have thought he'd want Seamus or Siobhan or one of those.

Ann He suggested Offa.

Helen Suggested what?

Ann Offa. Like the dyke. King Offa. He said it should be something easy to write in case he's non-literate.

Helen Make him Og then.

Ann Good idea. And Bert as a middle name. Then he can be Og or Ogbert depending on how well he does at school ... If I had a boy called Offa and a girl called Honour I'd have an Offa and Honour.

Helen He is coming back, is he?

Pause. Ann looks steadily at Helen

Terry?

Ann No, I don't think he is. If you must know.

Helen Ah.

Ann Yes, ah. Another problem to all get your teeth into.

Helen It's your problem.

Ann shakes her head

And that won't shake it away. Why didn't you tell us?

Ann I've just said why. Because you'll turn it into a big problem between you, make it terribly *important*.

Helen Isn't it?

Ann Mum'll get upset and start worrying, as if it's somehow her fault. And you two'll do a big production number on it, treat it like one of those Open University sociology programmes. *The Problems of the One-parent Family* ... I'm not a one-parent family and I'm not a casebook, I'm me and all I want to do is have my child ...

Ann suddenly burst into tears. Fox stands up. He is disconcerted. He crosses to the table. Ann is crying quietly after the first outburst, like a child on its own. Fox gives a slight gesture as if to touch her, but doesn't

Helen Mum's coming.

Ann looks up, then goes quickly, towards the end of the garden

Fox goes back to his chair

Mary comes out from the house with a tray of tea

I was going to get the tea.

Mary Kate made it. (*She puts the tray down and pours tea for them both*) Is Annie at the plums again?

Helen Yes.

Mary Oh, would you like some cake?

Helen Sit down, Mum.

Mary sits down. Pause

Mary I don't think it'll be long. (*Pause*) We can cut the grass.

Helen looks at her attentively

Do you think the house needs painting?

Helen I hadn't noticed. Maybe.

Mary It hasn't been done for years. It's flaking, do you see? The inside needs doing too. I noticed as I was coming downstairs. It looks quite shabby. One gets used to things ... Perhaps it's the sun.

Helen What?

Mary That makes things look shabby.
Helen Yes ...
Mary It all looks shabby, the furniture looks shabby. The stair carpet's nearly threadbare.
Helen You might move.
Mary Move?
Helen Somewhere smaller? You don't have to stay here.
Mary I shall be all right. I shall manage.
Helen Yes, I know.
Mary I suppose I could move. It hadn't occurred to me. I suppose I could do anything. Couldn't I?
Helen Anything you like.
Mary Go on a cruise ... Live in the country ... I could go on the streets.
Helen Nothing to stop you. You might find it's your métier.
Mary Mm.
Helen Kate told me John Parrish is going to look after things for you.
Mary Mm. Yes. He's been very helpful.
Helen How?

Pause

Mary I told Kate I hadn't seen him. That's not quite true. Well, it's not at all true.
Helen Mum, you don't have to tell me anything.
Mary Don't you want me to?
Helen Of course, if you want.
Mary He's been about for some years actually. He telephoned one day ... No he didn't. I phoned him. I heard he was back, so I telephoned. We met under the clock at Waterloo and had tea at Lyons Corner House.
Helen Lyons Corner House?
Mary No, it couldn't have been, could it? Somewhere ...

Pause

Helen Mum ...?
Mary He was a very good looking man in his day ... Your father. You've seen photographs.
Helen Yes.
Mary Not my type, though, really.

Helen looks at her

Wasn't that odd? My daydream was more the Nordic type. You know, tall, clean-limbed, square-jawed. It's the Welsh, I suppose. Short and dark—his hair was quite black, jet-black. Celts, are they? Picts? The early settlers. Before we moved in. Whoever we are. Angles, Danes, Saxons, Normans, Romans, we're bastards really, a bastard race. He must have been pure Celt or Pict or whatever. The Cornish are the same, aren't they? A very secretive race, very much inside ... But my word, the necessity ...
Helen What, Mum?

Mary He was a tail gunner.
Helen Yes, I know.
Mary Taffy the tail gunner. I was only seventeen. I found it quite mysterious, the idea of this little dark man crouched in the tail of his Wellington. Not romantic, just rather outlandish. He said it was like sitting in the toe of a boot. He still had his accent then. "It's only like sitting in the toe of a boot." And over Germany he'd fly in his boot and drop bombs on the towns while I was fast asleep in Godalming, not knowing anything about it. My parents distrusted him.

Slight pause

Helen Did they?
Mary *Mis*trusted him. There was something strange. He was like a bat. He'd appear and disappear again. Never seemed to settle. You could almost imagine him sleeping upside down from a rafter ... He seemed to have no roots, no interests ... Except me, for some reason. That— necessity. (*Pause*) He could have been Polish. You've heard about the Polish airmen? Only without the smile, he didn't smile much, he was very serious, not serious ... Intent. (*Pause*) There was nothing I had to give him. I don't think so. Just—accept his intensity. He seemed to be trapped in it. In himself, in his own intensity. Like a bat in an attic ... I don't know whether he stopped looking for it; whatever it was. Or if the intensity was just a blind thing. His lovemaking could be quite frightening. As if he were frantically beating against a door, dashing against it. It didn't change, but it became somehow mechanical ... He became a very good business man. He put his heart into it ... His heart went into it. (*Pause*) It was funny; seeing John again. I don't know what I expected. Not to start anything up again. I don't think so. It wasn't that kind of thing. It may have been that with John there *was* something I could give him, something very simple, and he was always so grateful. And there he was under the clock looking just the same as ever. So— gentlemanly, such a gentlemanly man ... He's been so kind. And so grateful. He has such an old-world way of saying thank you, it was so nice ...
Helen So you've seen a lot of him.
Mary Oh, yes, regularly. Every Tuesday.
Helen Why Tuesday?
Mary I don't know, dear. It's easier if there's a regular arrangement.

Pause

Helen Mum ...
Mary I'm sorry, am I upsetting you?
Helen No, of course not ...
Mary Isn't the garden looking lovely?
Helen Mum, do you mind if I stay here? For a while?
Mary No, why should I, I like having you here. What about your—centre?
Helen I don't think I can go back there. Not yet. They'll have to manage. They'll manage. No-one's indispensable.

Mary That's settled then ... Everything's all right, is it?

Pause

Helen I think what I really need at the moment is to have you say those things you used to say when I got difficult. It'll all look better in the morning. I expect you're run down. Why don't you take a laxative and go to bed? A nice hot bath and an early night.

Mary It usually helps.

Helen I know ... Mum, I have an awful feeling that something's gone disastrously wrong.

Mary With you?

Helen Not just me. With ... Look, I know I'm in a bad way, and you'll put it all down to that, to me feeling miserable and projecting it onto the world, and tomorrow I'll feel better and everything will seem fine, but what if it's not? What if it's the happy ones and the balanced ones who get the false view, what if it really *is* bad? What if—? Oh, I don't want to go on like this ...

Mary Go on, dear.

Helen All right. What if there's something *permanently* wrong, something that *can't* be put right, with—Oh, I hate these terms. Society, the world we've made. With *us*. With people. With *homo sapiens*. I know it sounds ridiculous, it sounds pseud, the kind of nihilistic wallowing adolescents get into. But if it's *fact*? Something irredeemably wrong, irremediably wrong. With us all, with it all ... Do I sound ridiculous?

Mary It's a thought.

Helen Oh, Mum ...

Mary What can I say, dear?

Helen You can tell me to have a nice hot bath and read a book. You can tell me to stop it. I've already upset Annie. Stop me.

Mary Even if it's true there's nothing you can do about it, is there?

Helen You sound like Annie.

Mary So it's surely best not to bother about it.

Helen And if I can't stop bothering about it? Because it won't go away if I stop bothering about it.

Mary Is there a man about at the moment?

Helen Mum, it's not that!

Mary I'm not saying it is. I'm only asking.

Helen Well, no, not really. No regular arrangements. The odd one. For therapeutic purposes. For relief.

Mary Not for enjoyment?

Helen I told Annie I didn't miss him. Mum, I've never stopped missing him. On top of everything I can't stop missing him, it's ridiculous, it's meaningless but I can't ... (*She breaks down*) And I'm bothering about *that*. People are killing each other, Mum, God knows what's going to happen, and I'm bothering about *that*. It's all such a waste. Oh, the waste of it all ... Stop me, Mum, it's not fair on you. Stop me ...

Fox stands up. He is taken aback

Kate appears

Kate Mum. Will you come?

Mary looks at her for a moment, then follows her into the house

Helen stands up, looking towards the house. While she still stands, Fox sits and speaks. Helen sits presently

Fox Asparagus is planted four or five inches deep, six or eight inches apart, the same between the rows, preferably in raised beds, though some say this is unnecessary if the ground is well dug and manured. It should be left for the first three years, simply kept weed-free and given a layer of farmyard manure each autumn and some say a sprinkling of industrial salt. After the third year cutting may begin, cutting the spears, some say, an inch or so beneath the surface, from April to June. Twenty five plants should produce a sufficiency for two people and the plants should be good for fifteen or twenty years ... The father put down asparagus. He studied the subject. He liked the idea of the three fallow years, followed by fifteen, twenty years, his lifetime probably, of cutting. This, we may assume, is the third year ... Oddly enough, perhaps, his thoughts, in odd lucid moments, have been not so much on business, wife, children, opportunities lost, a sense of intensity left without an object, who he is and where he is going, what is the meaning of it all; but more on the asparagus plants which, good for fifteen or twenty years crop of succulent spears, best eaten in the classic manner, boiled, with melted butter, may be left unweeded, unmanured, uncut ... The sun is lower still now, only just above the trees. Soon it will be gone—as we say; not really gone, of course, we go from it. In the United States, five hours behind on the East Coast, eight hours behind on the West Coast, it shines bright, though not on the shirt-sleeved—what does one call them, technicians, operatives?—below ground, who make their own light and air. One would expect them to be bemused. They are not. They are too well trained. Bemusement is not in their programme. They do what has been set out for them to do in such and such an eventuality.

Ann comes back from the end of the garden

Helen has stopped crying. Ann sits down

Ann I blubbed.
Helen It's a free country.
Ann Tea. There's the mater. In a difficult situation—tea.
Helen Don't make fun of her.
Ann I'm not. (*She pours herself some tea*) Why did I blub?
Helen You tell me.
Ann You're the expert.
Helen On blubbing?
Ann No, on—psychological motivation.
Helen Men work and women weep, don't you know that? Beside which, as I said before, my love, you're shit-scared.

Pause

Ann You think? (*Pause*) Did I hear Kate's dulcet tone?
Helen Yes.
Ann I knew it was either her or a cat on heat ... Have you ever dreamt you were flying?
Helen No. Falling downstairs.
Ann It's supposed to symbolise sex, isn't it? I mean flying, not falling downstairs. What does falling downstairs represent?
Helen Fear of falling downstairs.
Ann Why didn't I think of that? ... Did I tell you I've been reading it up?
Helen Psychology?
Ann Yes.
Helen I had guessed. Why?
Ann Oh, for the best reasons. Someone left a book in the loo ... I don't believe a word of it.
Helen I'll write and tell the Psychoanalytical Society.
Ann I don't ... That's known as affirmation by negation, isn't it?
Helen Clever girl.
Ann In other words I really believe it and I'm just kidding myself; which goes to show Freud was right.
Helen Why do you think you don't believe it?
Ann I choose not to.
Helen And the world's flat, of course.
Ann Oh, yes, that goes without saying ... They're all so earnest, aren't they? Pinning us all down, explaining us all away.
Helen That's a very superficial view.
Ann Put me right then.
Helen It's just another language. A way of describing reality.
Ann It's either true or not true.
Helen Any consistent language is a truth. Euclidean geometry is a truth. It's not the only kind of geometry.
Ann I never thought of that. And what good does it do?
Helen You're asking what good language is.
Ann Sometimes I wonder.
Helen So do I.
Ann As you say, there are more nuts about than ever ... I thought I'd go nutty reading about it ... If you live absolutely in the present there can't be any cause and effect, can there?
Helen What do you mean?
Ann Cause and effect's a time thing, isn't it? If you live in the now, it can't apply.
Helen Living's a time thing.
Ann Yes, but ... Oh ... I was on a hilltop with some Indians ...
Helen What?
Ann My dream. They were flying; stepping off the edge into thin air. It looked lovely. Only I was scared. My Indian said, "It's quite easy. Just raise your arms like this, take a step and let go. You can see it

works". And he stepped off and flew. So I thought, "What the hell". And *I* stepped off and flew. It was marvellous. You don't have to flap. You soar. If you want to go higher you just raise your arms a bit. Bank. Turn ... It was so real I can't believe it didn't happen. Every now and then I feel if I raised my arms and felt right, up I'd go ... What are you laughing at?

Helen I just got a mental image.

Ann I should be beautiful. I'd take all my clothes off, they'd flutter down into the sea ... Then I'd have my baby up there. It would come out and fly immediately, flit round me like a cherub ...

Helen What about the afterbirth?

Ann You are a prosaic cow ... You've got no poetry, that's your trouble. Your *problem*.

Helen Poetry flies, people don't. That's the problem.

Ann Hm. (*Pause*) I don't want to be scared.

Helen Who does?

Ann I'm not most of the time ... And if I am, that's all part of it, isn't it? I don't want to be scared of being scared. I want to accept it, accept everything. I want to open myself. Lay myself open. Not shut off. Not protect. Not dodge the issue.

Helen What issue?

Ann That we don't—know, do we, about anything. It's all uncertain, everything's uncertain, anything might happen any time. Whatever we do, we're vulnerable. Every minute. Well, that's what I want to be then. Vulnerable. Accepting that I'm vulnerable.

Helen And the baby?

Ann Yes, and the baby. I want it to grow up—naked. Knowing how naked it is ... It is possible to live like that, isn't it?

Helen I couldn't.

Ann Maybe I can. Don't you think?

Helen I don't know.

Ann Why do I feel like crying again? (*She looks down at her baby*) Why do I feel like crying, my love?

Kate comes out. She looks at them, sits down

Been having another shit?

Pause

Kate He stopped breathing. He's going again now. Mum wants to stay there.

Ann You say "going" like a watch.

Kate takes out a packet of cigarettes, offers it to Helen, who shakes her head. Kate lights a cigarette

Kate I've been thinking. I'm leaving Germany. I'm going to live here. For a while. I've got what I could out of Germany. I've done it ... Mum's going to be free. For the first time in her life really. She lived at home till she got married. She was the daughter, then she was the wife, then she

was the mother. She's been defined from outside all her life. Spent her
life as an appendage to other people; looking after other people. Living
stereotypes. Now she's free. She doesn't have to do that any more. She
mustn't. (*She looks at Ann*) You mustn't make her. She's not your
mother any more, not in that sense. She'll want to be, but you're not to
let her ... And she's not to settle down with that Parrish man. She's got
too much in her for that kind of life. She's lived hardly any of herself.
It's all potential. She's got to use it. She's got to be given the chance.
Helen To do what?
Kate It doesn't matter what she does. So long as she does it on her own
account, not on someone else's. We'll talk a lot, go to meetings, I'll find
some organisations ... I was watching her, sitting there with him. She
looked—lost. As if she didn't properly exist ... Waiting—She's never
been her own person, she's always lived on behalf of somebody else, it's
not fair!

Pause

Helen Do you mean you want somebody to look after?

Kate looks at her blankly

Ann I shan't give any trouble. I don't know what all the fuss is about. I'm
not asking anything of anybody; just to have my own baby in my own
house. If she wants to take an interest I'm not going to stop her. Just
because she's not a raving feminist self-realisation freak doesn't mean
she's not anyone. Maybe she *prefers* just to live her own life rather than
endless discussions on who she is and why she isn't and how to find her
real self and all that shit!

Pause

Helen He's not dead yet. Let's not fight over her.

Pause

Kate Sorry. It was a shock. He suddenly s-stopped. Sorry, Annie, I didn't
mean it the way it came out ... I am coming back though. They say
after five years abroad you have to make a decision which country you
belong to. Well, I've decided. Anyway, I've done what I wanted to.
Ann What was that?
Kate I've shown I could do it. Break away. Cut my roots. When I went
over there I didn't speak the language, I had no job, no friends. I'd left
the bloke I was in love with. I had to redefine everything about myself.
What it is to be a woman, to be in love, to be of a particular nationality.
I've learnt a lot about who I am.
Ann And where's it got you?
Helen Stop it, Annie.
Kate All right, it's got me back living at home. Only with a bit more
self-awareness.
Ann Back with Mummy.

Kate This time it's my decision.

Ann What difference does that make? The result's the same, isn't it? The same for you as for me. All this stuff about cutting yourself loose, finding who you are, all that shit? And who are you when it's finished? It's all a put-on. You've always known you had a rabbit run back here, back home. The same as me. And here you are. Back with Mummy.

Kate Why are you trying to get at me, Annie?

Helen (*quietly*) Stop it, children.

Pause

Kate My God, you look obscene with that thing sticking out.

Ann blows a raspberry

Ann Who knows? I may have a genius. I may have the new Messiah. Maybe it wasn't Terry but a Venusian, while I thought I was having a nice dream. The flying dream! While I was flying they were pumping me full of psychedelic sperm from another world. When he's four years old the Pope will sit at his feet and say: Yes, of course, that's how it is. Why didn't I think of that before?

Kate Or *her* feet.

Ann No. It's got to be a guy. A sexual superman, he'll fuck the way we talk. He'll wander the world in bare feet, fucking the multitudes, and the pill will be as a pinch of dust against the truth of his loins. He'll populate the world with golden people ... Won't you, my love?

Pause

Helen We don't need dreams, Annie. There've been too many dreams. God preserve us from more dreams.

Slight pause

Ann *I* know. Let's *all* live at home. It'll be like *The House of Bernarda Alba*. We can spend our lives hating each other and shrivelling up inside, till someone takes the knife out. Bags I first.

Ann sings softly

Mary appears

Helen and Kate look at her questioningly, but she seems not to notice. She sits down

Mary Is there more tea?

Kate picks up the teapot and shakes it

Helen I'll put some more water in.

Helen takes the teapot and goes into the house

Mary The last time we were all here in the garden together was the Easter of the barbecue.

Kate Yes, Mum.

Ann That disaster.

Kate looks sharply at Ann

Well, it was. You ought to remember, you were the one who yelled at everyone and burst into tears.

Kate Yes, all right, you don't have to bring that up now.

Ann Why not? What's the difference? It's all over. I don't see the point in bothering about things that have already happened. It's all over, isn't it, Mum? Mum understands. We understand each other. Don't we, Mum?

Mary Your father always found Good Friday disturbing. He never knew what to do with it. He hated Christianity for taking over the old festival. He felt they'd stolen it. Cheapened it, taken the easy way out. Because they all know on the Friday that it'll all be all right again on the Sunday. He said once he wished the sun would go out like it did in the Bible; that would give them something to think about. He'd moon about on the Friday, not knowing what to do with himself. He wouldn't drink. He'd go up to his room and listen to the St Matthew Passion with the curtains drawn. One year there was a cloudburst and the rain came through the ceiling up there and started dripping onto the bookshelves. He wouldn't move. He sat listening to the St Matthew Passion while the rain poured onto his books. He liked Easter Monday though. That was his pagan day.

Fox On the Monday in question he was drunk early. Jolly drunk, careless drunk. He felt unusually light-hearted and sociable. The pains, which he'd not mentioned, had let up. He lit his new barbecue badly and too late. Spilt dressing on his trousers. The meat, of which he'd bought too much, tasted of white spirit. It rained. He knocked the barbecue over. He finished on the grill. They ate in the kitchen. The pains started again.

Ann Those burnt offerings.

Mary Water over the mill.

Ann Yes, what does it matter? It's finished. It never did matter. Nothing matters. It's not real. What do you want, my love? Mum, feel (*She takes Mary's hand and puts it on her belly*) We could have one next weekend. Shall we, Mum? Next Sunday? Invite some people, and all get drunk in the sun. I feel like eating a surfeit of burnt flesh!

Pause. Kate puts her hands over her face, but sits still and silently

Helen comes from the house, without the teapot

Helen Mum ...

Mary Yes, I know, dear.

Helen looks at her, uncertain what to do. She sits down.

Ann looks up at the sky. The light has changed

Ann There goes our hydrogen bomb.

Ann sings softly

CURTAIN

FURNITURE AND PROPERTY LIST

ACT I

On stage: Garden table. On it: nearly empty wine bottle, four glasses, remnants of a cold meal, plates, cheese, radio with ear plug attachment. Four garden chairs

Off stage: Plums (**Ann**)
Paperback book (**Helen**)
Small paper bag containing a cold sausage (**Kate**)
Bottle of wine with corkscrew in cork (**Ann**)

Personal: **Helen:** cigarettes

ACT II

Off stage: Tray of tea things, pot, cups, milk jug (**Mary**)

Personal: (**Kate**): packet of cigarettes, lighter

LIGHTING PLOT

ACT I

To open: Exterior lighting, late afternoon sun

ACT II

To open: Exterior lighting, late afternoon sun—less bright than Act I
The light fades noticeably towards the end of the Act.

EFFECTS PLOT

Cue 1	**Helen** switches on the radio *Very loud pop music*	(Page 4)
Cue 2	**Helen:** "Sorry". She turns the radio down *Lower sound*	(Page 4)
Cue 3	**Ann:** "Get a better class of news on Four, do you?" **Helen** retunes dial *Effect of changing station to Radio Three and sound* *level adjusted*	(Page 4)
Cue 4	**Helen** plugs the ear plug into the radio *Sound of radio off*	(Page 4)
Cue 5	**Helen:** "Ssh!" *Sound of aeroplane passing overhead*	(Page 6)